OCEAN
FANTASIES COLORING BOOK

Aaron Pocock

Dover Publications, Inc.
Mineola, New York

This enchanting coloring book features thirty-one illustrations of fantastical ocean scenes. They include alluring mermaids, giant sea monsters, mythological gods, playful dolphins, and sunken treasure. Intended especially for the advanced colorist, these images will spark your imagination. The pages are perforated and printed on one side only for easy removal and display.

Copyright

Copyright © 2017 by Aaron Pocock
All rights reserved.

Bibliographical Note

Ocean Fantasies Coloring Book is a new work, first published by Dover Publications, Inc., in 2017.

International Standard Book Number

ISBN-13: 978-0-486-81799-6
ISBN-10: 0-486-81799-7

Manufactured in the United States by LSC Communications
81799701   2017
www.doverpublications.com